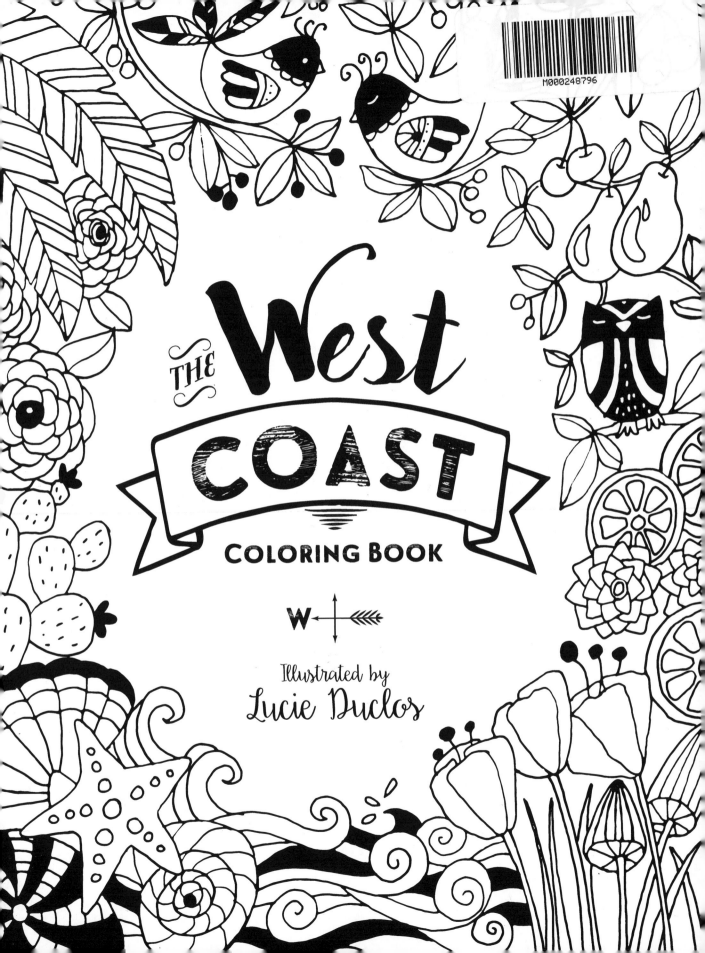

THE West COAST

COLORING BOOK

W

Illustrated by
Lucie Duclos

Published in April 2016
by Lucie Duclos Design
Port Townsend, Wa 98368
email: info@westcoastcoloringbook.com
www.westcoastcoloringbook.com

Designed and illustrated by Lucie Duclos
© 2016 Lucie Duclos

ISBN 978-0692671979

YOU ARE IN FOR A FUN & WILD
WEST COAST ADVENTURE...
ENJOY THE RIDE!

~ Lucie

"Relais Nature" a cookbook with recipes using sticks, twigs and other forest items.

"Blé d'Inde Band" by Lucie Duclos won an Honorable Mention at the Culinar Concours Communication Jeunesse.

Lucie and Mélina's first book: The PNW Coloring Book

ABOUT ME AND THIS BOOK

I've always liked to draw and make books. When I was about 10, my friend Sylvie and I created our first cookbook with delicious recipes made with things found in nature, like bark and leaves and spruce resin. We were surprised that we couldn't find a publisher as this was a very innovative concept for a cookbook at the time!

I grew up in Montreal and studied fine arts and graphic design in college. My favorite subject was illustration and one of our projects was to enter a children's book illustration contest. I won the Children's Honorary Mention Award, which I think was the best prize since real children actually voted for it.

After college, I worked for a magazine publisher in Montreal. I loved working with teams of writers, photographers and illustrators. When I moved to the San Francisco Bay Area, I freelanced for various magazines and catalogs. After I had my son, I decided to start my own kid's clothing business and then got into packaging design and surface pattern design.

I moved north to Port Townsend, Washington four years ago and this is really home to me. I love the weather and the beauty that surrounds this place. I especially enjoy the rain. When I was young, I used to spend my summers at our lake cabin up North in Quebec. My mom always planned craft activities for rainy days and I looked forward to hearing her say:

"On va faire de l'artisanat!" That's why I still love rainy days, because for me, they are loaded with potential and possibilities of craft projects!

For a longtime, I've had a dream of illustrating a children's book. When I published my first coloring book for adults with my friend Mélina last year, I realized that I just made my dream come true. We created a kids book, but for adults! **The Pacific Northwest Coloring Book**, was such a great adventure that I decided to make another one with a Pacific Coast vibe: **The West Coast Coloring Book**.

Rain or shine, it's time to get creative and start coloring! I hope you enjoy my new book!

Lucie

westcoastcoloringbook.com
pnwcoloringbook.com

lucie@duclosdesign.com
duclosdesign.com
snowflower at spoonflower.com
instagram:lucieduclos

West Coast CITIES

PORT TOWNSEND, CITY OF DREAMS

With its maritime heritage and artist spirit, Port Townsend was called the "City of Dreams" because of the early speculation that the city would be the largest harbor on the West Coast. When that didn't happen, a lot of Victorian buildings were abandoned and left untouched for nearly 100 years. The Port Townsend Historic District, was designated a National Historic Landmark in 1977.

SEATTLE, EMERALD CITY

Seattle was nicknamed "The Emerald City" mostly due to the lush, green forests of Washington and the more than 6,000 acres of parks within the city limits. On the Puget Sound, with the Cascade Range and Mount Rainier as a backdrop, Seattle is the largest city in the Pacific Northwest. The "futuristic" Space Needle is a legacy of the 1962 World's Fair.

PORTLAND, CITY OF ROSES

In the shadow of snow capped Mount Hood, Portland is known for its parks, bridges and bicycle paths, as well as for its eco-friendliness, creative spirit, indie vibe, coffeehouses and food truck scene. Roses also grow like crazy in Portland, check out the International Rose Test Garden while you are there.

SAN FRANCISCO PAINTED LADIES

"Painted Ladies" is a term in American architecture used for Victorian and Edwardian houses and buildings painted in three or more colors that embellish or enhance their architectural details. One of the best-known groups of "Painted Ladies" is the row of Victorian houses across from Alamo Square park, in San Francisco.

HOLLYWOOD GOLDEN ERA

The Golden era of Hollywood (1930's through the 1940's) was a time of glamour, prosperity and technological advances to the American Society. Most people were attending films at least once a week and about 800 films were being created a year. Classical Hollywood Style Cinema, developed from 1917 to 1960, characterizes most films to this day.

CORONADO ISLAND, SAN DIEGO

Hotel del Coronado is a historic beachfront hotel, just across the San Diego Bay. It is one of the few surviving examples of an American architectural genre: the wooden Victorian beach resort. When it opened in 1888, it was the largest resort hotel in the world. It has hosted presidents, royalty, and celebrities throughout the years.

West Coast ART AND CULTURE W+↤

CHIHULY BRIDGE OF GLASS

The Chihuly Bridge of Glass in Washington State is a 500-foot-long pedestrian overpass that links the Museum of Glass to downtown Tacoma, the hometown of internationally-renowned glass artist Dale Chihuly. His large and colorful glass sculptures and installations make you feel like you are in an underwater sea garden.

THE ARTS

The West Coast inspires many artists, writers, dancers, performers, singers and musicians. It is also home to a vast number of world-class museums, galleries, theaters, art schools and workshops for every skill level. And with the new coloring craze, everybody is diving in! So get your colored pencils out and start creating!

BOARDING CALL

The surfing culture in California is legendary. Surfers personalize their boards to reflect their personality and style. There are many types and shapes of surfboards to suit a specific type of wave or a surfer's skills. From longboard to shortboard, from fish to funboards or hybrid, the possibilities are endless. Surf's up!

MISSION SANTA BARBARA

Mission Santa Barbara is the home of the annual "I madonnari" chalk painting festival held over Memorial Day weekend. Street painters transform the mission plaza into 150 vibrant and colorful, large scale images. The festival benefits the Children's Creative Project, a nonprofit arts education program.

LIVE MUSIC

The West Coast has a vibrant music scene. From rock to classic, to blues, jazz and pop, there is a festival out there waiting for you. So many opportunities to listen to live music and to learn from the masters. Get out there and follow the music, you will find your rhythm.

TALAVERA MEXICAN TILES

Talavera Mexican tiles are a staple of Spanish Revival Architecture. They originated in 17th century Mexico with the arrival of the Spaniards. The name Talavera was given to honor the Spanish craftsmen, who were from the town of Talavera De La Reina, Spain, and introduced the new industry to Mexico.

West Coast LIFESTYLE W✝⟪⟪

HIKING THE PCT

Hiking the Pacific Crest Trail became very popular after the film 'Wild' in 2014. The PCT is a wild and scenic pathway from Mexico to Canada through California, Oregon and Washington. The route passes through 25 National Forests and 7 National Parks and through the highest portion of the Sierra Nevada and Cascade Mountain Ranges.

HAPPY CAMPERS

Whether you have a pup tent or a fully equipped camper, there are so many National and State Parks and Forests on the West Coast, that it might be hard to decide where to go. Make sure you don't leave any food out because you may be visited by many critters and probably a few hungry bears.

SURFIN' USA

"I've got a '34 wagon and they call it a woodie" sang Jan & Dean in the hit "Surf City" in 1963, making the "woody" forever part of the surf culture in Southern California. Surfing is more often described as a lifestyle than a sport. There are plenty of beaches if you want to catch a few waves on the West Coast!

ROAD TRIPPING

The famous winding Pacific Coast Highway offers spectacular views up and down the coast from San Francisco to San Diego. Travel over the Bixby Bridge to Big Sur, visit the majestic Hearst Castle in San Simeon or stroll through the beautiful streets of Santa Barbara.

SKI IN THE WEST

There is great skiing in the west, not right on the coast but not too far either. You can go to the beach and ski in the same day. From Mammoth to Lake Tahoe, to Mount Hood, and Mount Baker, get your skis or snowboard out and hit the slopes' fluffy white powder!

EXPLORING THE PARKS

If you like to tour National Parks and Monuments, you've come to the right place! Some are open in the summer only, some are open all year round, all are stunningly beautiful and feature spectacular coastline, scenic lakes, majestic mountains and glaciers, and magnificent rainforests.

West Coast WILDLIFE AND NATURE W⊣⋘

SEASHELLS AND TIDE POOLS

Up and down the West Coast there are miles and miles of beaches and on them, seashells everywhere: clams, oysters, mussels, scallops, dogwinkles, etc. Go beachcombing or tide pooling and see what kind of treasures you can find. And if you are lucky, you might find some sea glass too. Low tide is the best time to go.

WHALE WATCHING

Whale watching is a popular pastime on the West Coast. In some locations, you can even see whales spouting, breaching, and fluking from ocean bluffs or even from a ferry. Some of the species you will encounter on the Pacific Coast are grey whales, orcas, humpbacks, minkes and gigantic blue whales.

KELP FOREST

The West Coast is home to many harbor seals. They are very playful and love to lay in the sun on the warm sandy beaches or on rocks and piers along the coast. Once in a while you catch them swimming through the kelp forest in search of their favorite mermaid.

SALMON RUN

Salmon spend their early life in rivers, and then swim out to sea where they live their adult lives and gain most of their body mass. When they have matured, they return to the rivers to spawn. In the west, you will find species like Pacific king, chinook, coho, sockeye and steelhead.

NATIVE BIRDS

This whimsical bird can only be found in this book. I looked for them in the wild, but wasn't able to find one, probably due to their elusive and shy nature. If you see one, please make sure to send me a picture at info@westcoastcoloringbook.com

THE REDWOODS

The magnificent Redwoods are some of the tallest and oldest trees on earth. Coast Redwoods only grow in one place on Earth, right here on the Pacific Coast, from Big Sur to southern Oregon. They can grow to 300 feet or more and live for thousands of years.

West Coast GARDENS AND FORESTS W↕«

CACTUS COLLECTION

Most of the West Coast has a great climate to grow cacti and succulents and most people have some in their gardens. They come in all sorts of shapes and sizes and have names like prickly pear, barrel, saguaro, beaver tails, echeveria, agave, aloe, hedgehog and rosularia.

FANCY FOREST

Ready for a stroll through an imaginary forest? You won't find a lot of the trees you see on this page walking through the woods, but you will find a lot of other species, from deciduous to evergreens, the West Coast has a wide range of trees of all shapes and sizes. Time for a forest bath!

CALIFORNIA POPPIES

This colorful and cheery wildflower was selected as the California state flower in 1903. It looks very delicate and fragile but it is actually quite drought tolerant and tenacious. You will encounter their bright orange blooms on hillsides everywhere in the Golden state and beyond.

FROM THE ORCHARDS

Washington, Oregon and California are a bounty of fresh fruits and vegetables. You will pass through fields, orchards and farms along the way and you can stop at produce stands by the roadside or shop at your local farmers market. Either way, you are in for a treat!

FUNGI AND FUN LEAVES

Yes, fungi are fun! They always make me happy when I spot one. Unlike plants, mushrooms do not contain chlorophyll and do not require sunlight to grow but they do need moisture so you will find them more in the Northwest or during the rainy season in the southern West Coast.

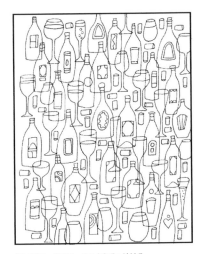

FROM THE GRAPEVINE

Oh, the wonderful nectar you can make from grapes! Red, rosé, white or bubbly, you will be able to find something for your taste buds if you go wine tasting at a local vineyard in one of the many wine regions on the West Coast, like Columbia Valley, WA, Willamette, OR or Sonoma, CA.

THANK YOU

I would like to thank my husband,
Dave Parisse, for his invaluable input,
amazing patience and constant support.
I love you Dave!

Et un gros merci à Mélina Lamoureux for
creating the first book with me and for
bouncing ideas back and forth on my first
solo book venture, you are awesome!

STAY IN TOUCH

Share your colored pages on social media!
#westcoastcoloringbook

westcoastcoloringbook

The West Coast Coloring Book

www.westcoastcoloringbook.com
info@westcoastcoloringbook.com

FROM THE SAME AUTHOR

$\mathcal{F}$or all lovers of the **Pacific Northwest**, this book offers **40 beautiful illustrations** by Lucie Duclos and Mélina Lamoureux, just waiting for you to add color. So get cozy, grab a cup of coffee and your favorite colored pencils and travel up and down the West Coast through luscious forests, seaside villages, serene lakes, snow capped mountains, salty oceans and white sandy beaches. You will certainly catch a few waves, hop on a ferry, sail to an island, watch for whales, visit a lighthouse and encounter all kinds of wildlife. A road trip through the Pacific Northwest for your inner artist!

www.pnwcoloringbook.com
instagram: pnwcoloringbook
#pnwcoloringbook

Made in the USA
San Bernardino, CA
18 May 2018